ALTARS

ESTABLISHING YOUR PRIESTHOOD

AYEISHA KIRKLAND

7-Day Developmental Devotional

I have three dedications for this book.

First, to the **Kingdom of God**,

I dedicate this book to your advancement.

This is for the honor of Almighty God and

the spreading of

the Gospel of Jesus Christ.

It was written through the inspiration of

The Holy Spirit.

Second, to two dynamic prayer warriors,

a woman who covers me in prayer as a

mother in the spirit,

Prophetess Sasha McDonald-Creary

and the writer of this book's Foreword,

Jephthe Odajuste.

Your prayer altars before the Lord deeply

inspired me to build one of my own. The

times you guys joined me in prayer left me

stirred to stay at His feet.

Third, to the gatekeepers of South Florida such as, **Elder Sally Mishkin, Pastor Carol Fleming,** and **Pastor Cheryl Sejour.** Your dedication to strategically praying for revival in Florida for decades gave birth to what I am experiencing right now. I am grateful.

Acknowledgements

Allow me to express my deepest gratitude for every person that played a role in the publication of this book:

Inspired by:

The Holy Spirit

Edited by:

Scribing Life Book Services

Copy Edited by:

Jerod Bellamy & Ingrid Cruickshank

Cover Designed by:

All Things Cre8

Back Cover Photo by:
Musiqool Media

Special Thanks To

1. My Mother, **Ingrid Cruickshank** for her selfless dedication to my godly upbringing and her constant support of my Kingdom calling.

2. **New Alpha Worship Center** for its constant support, love, and prayer.

3. **Apostle Errol and Pastor Angela Williams**, my spiritual father and mother. I am a product of their yes.

4. **Christian Williams,** my men-

tor who constantly pours into me, and **Niketa Williams-Cherilus,** whose obedience to the prophet- ic call on her life made this book possible.

5. **Ken Isidore**, for always being there for me.

Foreword

BY JEPHTHE ODAJUSTE

The principle and revelation of the altar goes as far as the times of Noah and is as relevant as New Testament described salvation. It is also used to describe salvation in the book of Hebrews. When men wanted to call upon the name of the Lord, they erected an altar. When men wanted to offer a sacrifice unto God, they erected an altar. When men encountered God, they erected an altar.

The altar is more than just a place of religious activity and practice. It is the evidence of functional priesthood. It is the sign of a lively and active relationship between God and man. Being that we are called a royal priesthood in Christ Jesus, we understand that altars are spiritual realities and not merely physical locations (1 Peter 2:9 & Revelation 5:10). Meaning that many things in the old covenant have transited to their full potential in the new, which is in the Spirit.

Now, being that Jesus is called our high priest in the Spirit and we are also called a royal priesthood in Christ, that can only mean one thing: the way Christ is officiating an altar of ever continuing intercession on our behalf, we are also called to raise up spiritual altars through prayer, worship, and the word that will eventually affect everything and everyone around us (Hebrews 4:14).

The believer bears many titles in Christ and one of them is that of "the royal priest". So if the principle of priesthood and the altar is as relevant as salvation, then there is a serious need to peep into the old, from the standpoint of the new, to have a concise understanding of what we now have in Christ Jesus. Until we do so, there are certain things that we will not experience in our relationship with God, the present day church, and the world.

I encourage you to journey through this devotional with every bit of hunger, expectation, and desire to see your spiritual life take a drastic shift for the good. This devotional will further explain priesthood to you as a quality of Christianity that evidently makes God known in your midst. I can assure you that my dear sister is one whose altar is not cold, but just like Leviticus 6:13, fire is kept burning on her altar. So open your heart, open your mind, and enjoy this devotional!

Your brother in Christ,
Jephthe Odajuste
Author, *The Man That Prays*

Contents

Introduction

For the majority of my living, I have had a front row seat to **Kingdom Culture**- the norms, customs, and mannerisms expressed by those who are followers of the doctrine of the Lord Jesus Christ (Matthew 4:23). Many people ignorantly believe that Christianity is just a religion, but it is more than a set of rules observed by church attendees. Instead, the rules in our Bible are more like a **constitution**. Every book in the Bible serves as founding documents of a government entitled the **Kingdom of God**. We are not just church-goers; instead, we are **Kingdom Citizens** with a responsibility to be God's **ambassadors** on Earth. As a result of our occupation, the book of Genesis-or the book of all beginnings- explains two major components of our job description.

The first one is **dominion:**

> And God said, Let us make man in our image, after our likeness: and let them have dominion over the fish of the sea, and over the fowl of the air, and over the cattle, and over all the earth, and over every creeping thing that creepeth upon the earth
>
> Genesis 1:26 KJV

As an ambassador on Earth, we are required to be a reflection of the One who sent us. For example, when a diplomat visits another country, they are not just a voice for their country, but a reflection of that country and its leader- their **King**. As an ambassador for God, we are required to be a reflection of God. God the Father and the Son do not live in this land. They are seated in Heaven; God is looking to us to be the execution of His standards on Earth while He is not here (Ephesians 2:6 & John 14:12). The believer is the presence of God on Earth, by letting the God in them (The Holy Spirit) shine through them (Romans 8:9). We are made in His image as a spirit because we are His mirror (John 4:24; 1 Thessalonians 5:23). Our God is a God of dominion.

Jesus has all authority in Earth and in Heaven (Matthew 28:18). As His reflection, we have authority over everything on Earth because without it, we cannot dominate the way He has called us to (Luke 10:19).

The second one is **opposition:**

> Now the serpent was more subtil than any beast of the field which the "Lord God had made. And he said unto the woman, Yea, hath God said, Ye shall not eat of every tree of the garden?
>
> Genesis 3:1 KJV

There is no need for dominion if opposition is absent. Dominion is only necessary when one is competing for territory.

We do not need power to obtain the world if we are the only ones who want it. For example, a country does not need an army to fight for a land if they are the only ones who desire to be in it, but that is not the case for us. Before we got here, a serpent, whose name is Satan, was cast down to the Earth (Revelation 12:7). He is a king as well (Ephesians 2:2). He is the ruler of the **Kingdom of Darkness.** His kingdom is actively fighting against the Kingdom of God to obstruct us from being the fulfillment, advancement, and expansion of God's Kingdom Culture (Revelation 12:17). His kingdom is the polar opposite to our Kingdom (Galatians 5:17).

How Does The Kingdom Of God Work?

The Kingdom of God is not like a traditional kingdom of this world (John 18:36). This is not about an election or a traditional passing of power through a family lineage. The Kingdom of God operates through three anointings: that of the King, Prophet, and Priest. Many people think these anointings function outside of one another, but really, they are dependent upon each other. God told His people through Moses the Prophet that He has made them a **Kingdom of Priests** (Exodus 19:6). For now, a priest is the one who serves in the presence of God. As we go into the devotional, we will discuss this position more in depth. The concept of a King-Priest model is emphasized in the New Testament. Peter the Apostle describes us as a **Royal Priesthood** (1 Peter 2:9). John the Apostle, later Elder, and eventually the Revelator, pronounces that God made us **Kings and Priests** (Revelation 1:6). Why are these two anointings placed together by Moses, Peter, and John? It is because they are not distinct from one another. Since our dominion comes from God, we cannot dominate as kings unless we serve in the presence of God as priests **first**. Before Jesus was positioned as King, He took the seat of the Great High Priest (Hebrews 9:11). If He did not execute a slaughter on an **altar called a cross** as a Priest, there is no way He would be seated far above every principality and power as the King of kings (Philippians 2).

The anointing of the prophet is a by-product of serving as a priest. Because Jesus stayed in the presence of God as a Priest, He was perfectly positioned to receive instruction from God through prophetic intelligence: the obtaining of information through prophetic channels, also known as Word of Knowledge (John 5:30; Isaiah 50:4). In simplest terms, because He served in the presence of God as a Priest, He could hear as a Prophet. Because He obeyed what He heard as a Prophet, He was able to dominate as The Most High King. As the King of kings, He expects for us to follow His example and operate in the anointing of a priest and prophet, so we can dominate as kings like He did (Revelation 19:6). This is what being made in the image of God is all about!

As you read this book, my desire is for you to obtain kingship. As you take this one week journey, I want you to obtain the tools necessary to come into the fullness of your kingly anointing. I want you to hear what God has been trying to say to you by resurrecting your prophetic anointing and unclogging those prophetic channels. That does not happen until you awaken your priestly anointing, and there was never a priest who did not have an altar built before the Lord. Get ready! It is time to build a ladder that will help you ascend into your purpose. Every day is a step into greater dominion.

****NOTE****

Each day will have an assigned scripture. Read that BEFORE starting the devotional. After the devotional, there will be reflection questions. Set aside ample time so you can jot responses to those questions. Each day will end with a prayer. This is just a starting point for intercession! It is NOT the sum total of your prayer for the day. Use it as a foundation to build upon and attempt to increase your prayer time daily.

Name Change

DAY 1: GENESIS 17

5Your name will no longer be Avram [exalted father], but your name will be Avraham [father of many], because I have made you the father of many nations.

Genesis 17:5 CJB

Names are important. You are not given a name to merely exhibit your parent's creativity; instead, names are essential to your identity. Because your name is what people call you, your name reveals what is associated with you. The moment someone mentions a name, you begin to imagine the person: how they look, how they sound, and more. The most supreme example of this is God. When He was building relationships with different people in the Bible, He revealed Himself through different names (Exodus 6:3). You call Jireh when you need a provider. You call Nissi when you need a protector. You call Shalom when you need peace. The list goes on. Names evoke adjectives. For this reason, God constantly changed people's names in the Bible when He was doing a new thing in their life.

Saul had to be called Paul. Simon had to be called Peter. Jacob had to be called Israel. Abram had to be called Abraham. New names are significant of a new season. When a bride is married to her husband, she takes on a new name: his name. When we get to heaven, a new place, we will be given a new name as His bride (Revelation 2:17; Revelation 3:12; Ephesians 5:22). When God does something new in you, He gives you a new name.

A Change Of Name = A Change Of Title

I am not telling you to run to the court house and spend money on a brand new name. The name is a symbol for a change in your title. The same way a name evokes adjectives, a title evokes adjectives. A manager has a different set of adjectives from a janitor. Many of the names we focus on in the Bible are simply titles that indicate where the character is from. Mary Magdalene was from Magdala and Jesus of Nazareth was from Nazareth. As you go to different, or deeper, places in your spirituality, a new name or title will be given to reflect the shift you are experiencing. David is an example of this. He was always David, but he transitioned from a shepherd boy to an armor bearer. Later, he became a military commander, and eventually, the king of Israel.

The first day of this devotional is a commencement of a new thing in you. As a result, a new name needs to be given to you.

You are no longer just a "church-goer". You are not merely a Kingdom Citizen. From now on, you need to know that you are a

PRIEST

The foreword and introduction perfectly describes that God has called us to be Priests. If you have not read it, please go back and see it before we move further. If you have read it, let us dig deeper. Understand that the priesthood is

An Old Testament Office

In Exodus 28, God establishes the office of the Priest through the Levitical lineage of Aaron. At that time, it was a monarch-type order that passed through a single bloodline from generation to generation. They were the **only ones** allowed to go in the presence of God and even handle the Ark of the Covenant (a physical symbol of the presence of God). They were responsible to make animal sacrifices to reconcile man back to God.

A Body Of Christ Responsibility

Even though the priesthood was established during the time of the law, it extended even into the grace period. Hebrews 9 explains that Jesus honored the law by being both a Priest and a sacrifice by offering Himself for the reconciliation of us back to God. As explained in the foreword and introduction (again read it if you have not!), the ministry of the Priest does not end with Christ, but continues with us through the royal priesthood. Old Testament practices become New Testament principles because God is the same yesterday, today, and forevermore. While we may not do the same exact practices today (i.e. animal sacrifices), we still have a responsibility to live out the principles (i.e. flesh sacrifices; Romans 12:1). As a result, we must fully understand what this office is, including its origin.

A Practice From Genesis

The first time that an actual Priest is mentioned is with Abram in Genesis 14. It is reiterated in Hebrews 7. In short, Abram gave his sacrifices to a Priest named Melchizedek (who later was called the King of Salem!). By offering sacrifices himself, Abram exercised priesthood.

It is important to understand that even though the priesthood office was established during the law, the principle of the Priest predates the law and extends into our time today as modernized disciples. It is not an outdated principle.

How Do I Function As A Priest?

Abram and Abraham have two different meanings. Abram means the exalted father. The word exalted is often associated with pride and humility (Matthew 23:12). Before Abram met God, he was called or known as an exalted father with no son. Read that carefully. Abram was known as an exalted father (a person giving birth to things in the earth) with no Son (Jesus Christ). We all share that same testimony. Before we met Jesus, we exalted ourselves.

We produced things in the Earth without His input or acknowledgement. This is an anti-priesthood lifestyle.

The crazy thing is, Abram's name did not change immediately after he started building a relationship with God. It did not even change when he sacrificed through Melchizedek. This is because, although he knew God, he still exalted himself. He still went to Egypt and lied about his marital status when God did not tell him to. He still went to Hagar to have Ishmael when God did not tell him to. Just because you start the process of knowing God, or you start making sacrifices to Him, it does not mean you have adopted the priesthood. The priesthood is not merely about giving God stuff, like the tenth Abram gave to Melchizedek. It is about sacrificing yourself. This is why Jesus is a prime example of the priesthood. Every time a Priest in Aaron's lineage entered the presence of God, they put their lives on the line. The altar was the place where they killed things. Understand that an **altar** is a **place of death:** where things die, where your flesh dies, and where you die. That requires you to become humble.

No longer could Abram be called an exalted father, because that exaltation was without a son and the Son (Isaac and Jesus). It was an inaccurate description of his current status and destiny. Also, it was a testimony of a lack of dependency. His new name, Abraham means a father of a multitude or many nations. No longer was he exalted. When you come into contact with the true "Son", you must come low

(Philippians 2:10). You must cut yourself. This is what the circumcision Abraham engaged in after represents. He killed his own flesh. He became a Priest. Once he was willing to sacrifice himself (as seen when he cut off the foreskin of his house and himself), he was able attain his actual son (Isaac). Compared to his sacrifice to Melchizedek, it was no longer an act of giving away stuff, but a lifestyle of sacrificing himself. He was so priestly that he did not even mind laying Isaac down as a sacrifice in Genesis 22. Even though God asked for Isaac, He did not want Isaac's life, He really wanted Abraham's heart. God does not want your stuff. God wants to make sure your stuff does not have you. In the end, it was the priesthood of Abraham that enabled him to dominate as the father of many nations. The life of Abraham shows the function of three anointings. He heard as a prophet and obeyed the instruction of God. He reigned as a king by being a father of many nations. However, the root of his success was really because he established a priesthood. He had an altar of death and he sacrificed himself. He humbled himself before God. God wants to do the same with you.

Incorporating This Into Your Prayer Life

As you build an altar before the Lord, allow him to change your identity. Lay down all of you. Vocally call out every desire you have for yourself, and ask God if that is in His plan for your life. Mention every area of your life and ask for His feedback. Divorce your preconceived notions for your own life and allow God to prophetically speak over you. Have some pen and paper to write down what you hear Him say.

Reflection Questions

1. What is my current name or title right now? Am I just a church-goer, a kingdom citizen, or a Priest?

2. What actions do I need to exercise to begin or extend my priesthood based on what I read in this chapter?

3. In what ways have I not been humble before God. What parts of my flesh do I have to sacrifice?

Prayer

Heavenly Father, I want to be a reflection of you on the Earth. I want to be a Priest before you. I build an altar before you. On this altar, I desire to crucify my flesh. Show me the areas in my life, through your Spirit, that need to die so I can be what you have called me to be. I present myself as a living sacrifice to you. One that you can have your way with. Convict me by your Spirit. This prayer must be more than words of my mouth. Instead, it must be the posture of my heart. I follow your lead. I look for your help. You alone be glorified in my life and heart.

In Jesus Name, Amen.

Face Change
Day 2: EXODUS 34:28-35

[29]When Moshe came down from Mount Sinai with the two tablets of the testimony in his hand, he didn't realize that the skin of his face was sending out rays of light as a result of his talking with [*Adonai*].

Exodus 34:29 CJB

People define Moses as a prophet only. They claim that Aaron is the only one considered a Priest during this time. They also think that an actual king did not come until Samuel anointed Saul. I disagree with this sentiment. Moses was not merely defined by the anointing of the prophet. He walked in all three anointing described in the introduction: a king and a prophet, stemming from being a Priest. When Aaron offered his first sacrifice in Leviticus 9, Moses went with him into the presence of God. Recall that a priest was a limited office. The Priest was the only one who went into the presence of God. The people could not go on their own. Even with its limitations, Moses was allowed to go in with Aaron. Moses operated as a Priest despite not being assigned the title.

This is symbolic of how we ought to function in our priesthood. We may not be an assigned Priest under the Old Testament law, but we also have access into the presence of God (also known as the Most Holy Place)(Ephesians 2:18). We have our own priesthood that is critical for us. Without it, we cannot function as prophets and kings. It was the priesthood of Moses that allowed him to hear and speak as a prophet. It was also how he dominated as a king, or the leader, of the Children of Israel.

Priest = Presence

Like Melchizedek, Moses operated as a Priest before the actual Levitical priesthood was established. They did not serve in the Most Holy Place in a Tabernacle or a

Temple, but they still made sacrifices on an altar. An altar is not just a physical object in a place of worship. **Building an altar before the Lord is a spiritual practice that reflects a humble, sacrificial posture (Romans 12:1).** When you build an altar, you acknowledge, invite, attend to, and thereby, manifest His presence.

When Aaron and Moses offered the first sacrifice, the fire of God came down and consumed it. This is symbolic of His Presence: "For our God is a **Consuming Fire**" (Hebrews 12:29). Priests constantly enter in and invite the presence of God. They **manifest** or make known the presence of God. While God may be omnipresent, His presence is not felt or experienced everywhere. It is only experienced where it is acknowledged and sought after. The Priest acknowledges and seeks after the presence of God.

PRESENT FOR PRESENCE

In order to experience the presence of God, you have to make yourself present before Him. This is why the Priest stood at the altar. They offered or **presented** themselves. In order to be present in one place, you have to be absent everywhere else. When Moses decided to go into the presence of God in Exodus 34, He went up on a mountain. Mountains are spiritually symbolic (you can read more about this in Chapter 5 of my first book: *Unlocking The Joshua Anointing*). They resemble separation. Moses departed himself from everyone and everything else to enter into the presence of God. This is called making room. Making room for God invites Him to fill up your space with all of who He is.

The presence of God comes with a present: the gift of Himself. While there are many components to this, the primary aspect of the gift of God is the gift of His word. God is His Word (John 1:1). While we have our Bibles, the presence of God gives us His **proceeding** **Word:** what God is saying right now (Matthew 4:4). This is the prophetic channel that comes out of the priesthood. It includes revelation of what God has already said (such as in your Bible) but, more so, future instructions. Although they may not be written yet, these future instructions **must** align with the Bible. It is imperative to understand that God's word is the foundation of everything else He does (Matthew 16:18).

He will not give you a prophetic message that contradicts His word (John 12:49).

Stay Here To Hear And Adhere

A Priest stays here (where God is) to hear (what God said). A Priest refuses to not see or hear from God. They also obey what they heard! If we want to operate in our priestly anointing, we have to be present with God and absent everywhere else. We have to refuse to go a day without seeking after Him and hearing from Him. Then, we need to change our lives to observe or adhere what God tells us to do. "Altar" is a homophone word (words that sound alike but are spelt differently). It is homony-mous with the word alter: change. An altar is really a place of alteration. Not only is it a place where we sacrifice unto God and ultimately interact with God, but it is also a place where we change because of God. The change occurs as a result of speaking with God; it is a by-product of hearing and adhering (obeying) what God said (Hebrews 4:12).

This is why Moses' entire face changed in the presence of God. It became white. White is symbolic of purity. In the presence of God, Moses became pure. His face is also symbolic: it includes his eyes, nose, and mouth. Eyes mean prophetic vision. Nose means prophetic discernment. Mouth means prophetic speech. He can see, discern, and speak purely or *clearly*. The change was so noticeable, the people around him responded in fear or *reverence*. He was able to dominate over them because of the alteration He experienced at the altar. The same should be said about us. We should present ourselves to Him so He can give us the present of Himself. We need to be here, to hear and adhere. We need to be altered at the altar. It will allow us to dominate in the Earth because they will see the change in our faces.

Incorporating This Into Your Prayer Life

As you build an altar before the Lord, be open to experiencing change in your nature. First, be here. Figure out times where you can be absent everywhere else so you can be present with God at your altar. Write down a schedule this week for your prayer time. Second, hear. Ask God what should change about you. Have a notebook to write down what He says. Begin to build bible study plans around subject areas you need to alter (ie. pride, lust, jealousy, etc.). Adhere is the most important. If you are a hearer but not a doer, you are deceiving yourself (James 1:22). Begin to put these things into practice.

Reflection Questions

1. When was the last time I presented myself before God? How often do I do this? Am I satisfied or can I do more? In what ways can I start or increase this in my schedule?

2. How should my life be altered at the altar? What needs to change about me so I can operate in Kingdom dominion?

Prayer

Heavenly Father, I really want to spend time with you. Give me the wisdom on how to seek you as much as possible. Reveal to me and help me cut off the areas of my life where I need to be absent, so I can be more present with you. Give me the present of you. I want to hear your voice and be changed by your word. I want to see, discern, and speak purely and clearly. Speak Lord, for I am here, listening. I make room for you.

In Jesus name, Amen.

Press Beyond

Day 3: 2 CORINTHIANS 3:12-18

14 What is more, their minds were made stonelike... for to this day the same veil remains over them

2 Corinthians 3:14 CJB

Yesterday, we spoke about the reason for the veil. The veil was something that began with Moses to hide his face from the people. The glory of God that altered his face, after he got out of the presence of God, was too overwhelming for them. Eventually, the same veil became a curtain that kept people out of the presence of God (Exodus 26:33). Only the priest could enter through the curtain (Hebrews 9:7). This means that access to the presence of God was limited. The curtain was the barrier that kept people out.

The veil is so much more than a cloth. It is symbolic of the spiritual separation between God and man caused by sin.

Sin: The Greatest Separation

Sin separates you from God (Isaiah 59:2). When Adam and Eve sinned, they caused death, or separation, between them and God (Romans 5:12). The greek word for life in the Bible is *Zoe* and it means the **abundant life of God that comes from connection to God** (John 10:10). If you are separated from God by sin, you lose that life as a result (Romans 6:23). It is a spiritual death. This is how Adam and Eve died in Genesis 3 after eating the fruit from the tree of Knowledge of Good and Evil. They were no longer connected to the life source, so they became spiritually dead (John 14:6). This spiritual death actually passed down to all mankind who were born after them, including us (Romans

5:14). What I am trying to say is, sin is a veil. It is a curtain that separates you from the presence of God.

No wonder the Serpent wanted Adam and Eve to eat the fruit in Genesis 3. He deceived them so they could lose His presence. This is why they got kicked out of the garden of Eden (Genesis 3:24). The Devil knows that a person out a place cannot fulfill their assignment (You can read more about this in Chapter 4 of my book: *Unlocking The Joshua Anointing*). If you lose His presence, you lose your altar. If you lose your altar, you lose your priesthood. Your prophetic and kingly anointing leave with it.

For many people, they have trouble understanding this concept. They ask, "Does God walk away from me when I sin?". The verse does not say "Your sin caused God to leave you". Instead it says, "your sin separated you from Him". Your sin pushes you away from God. Consider the feeling of not wanting to go to church after you did something wrong. That is a small sign of how sin opens a door that causes us to drift away from God. If you study the Bible closely, you will see that God never left the children of Israel. They were the ones who left Him. He kept sending prophets to seek after them, but they ignored His voice to entertain their sin. God was not the One who needed to repent or go back to them (Numbers 23:19). Instead, we are the ones called to repent or go back to Him. This is the thing about sin. Yesterday, we said to be present with God, you have to be absent from everything else. Sin makes you present with everything else and absent from God.

Press Beyond The Veil

Remember, the veil is not just a curtain but a symbol. On the first day, we mentioned that we are the bride of God that takes on His Name after we are joined to Him. Brides wear a veil. They hide themselves until the appointed time to come to their groom. The groom removes the veil.

After Jesus died on the cross, the Bible purposely mentions that:

> [51] Suddenly, the curtain of the sanctuary was torn in two from top to bottom, the earth quaked, and the rocks were split. [52] The tombs were also

opened and many bodies of
the saints who had fallen
asleep were raised

Matthew 27:51-52 CSB

Our Groom and Priest, Jesus Christ, removed our veil. The fact that there was no longer a curtain in the temple meant that His presence was no longer selective, but accessible. Let me make this absolutely clear. The veil did not tear when people stopped sinning, but **it tore when He died**. If access to His presence was dependent on being sinless, then nobody would have access. When we sin today, we do not put the curtain back up. Christ split the veil permanently. When we sin, we turn our back on a split curtain. We open our ears to the voice of the enemy and allow the shame and guilt to keep us away from the split curtain.

Even though the curtain split when Jesus died, I asked myself, **"how many people were unaware because they never turned (REPENTED) to look"**. This is the mystery that Paul described in 2 Corinthians 3. He said, "whenever a person turns to the Lord, the veil is removed" (2 Corinthians 3:16 CSB). The veil was ripped ever since Jesus died, but until you turn and see that it is no longer there, you will still allow sin to separate you.

This is for the people who have not been in His presence for a long time. Maybe it feels better to be present with your worldly desires. Maybe you have been wanting to come back but you are afraid that, if you go, you will find a curtain keeping you out.

Maybe you feel too angry, too lustful, or too sinful to even be in His presence because you are mad at Him and His people. God will not turn you away (John 6:37). There is no curtain separating you from your altar. You have zero excuses.

Just be genuine with God. Hebrews 4 reminds us that Christ is sympathetic; more specifically, He knows how you feel and what you go through. You do not have to hide from Him, but boldly seek after Him when you need Him (Hebrews 4:16). What I love about Moses and that veil is, he put it on for people but took it off before God. In front of people, he hid himself. Before God, he became naked. Adam and Eve did the opposite in their sin. They hid from God and tried to clothe themselves from God. They did not realize that God would see right through those leaves. **He sees right through you.** The presence is for you as well. It does not matter how long it has been since you have been there, or what is stopping you from going there. Turn to Him and let the veil be removed. The enemy is telling you not to go. This is only because he abhors what the presence of God will make you into.

Reflection Questions

1. What veils am I wearing before God? What sins are keeping me away from God? What feelings am I trying to mask from God?

2. When did I stop prioritizing His presence? What lie did I believe from the enemy at that point?

What truth from God counter-
acts that lie?

Incorporating This Into Your Prayer Life

As you build an altar before the Lord, do not let sin separate you from it. Do not let guilt and shame after sin cause you to desert your altar. Every time you fall, run to your altar. Approach the throne of grace boldly. Repent, and ask God to give you biblical strategy to combat against your sins. Read Psalms 51 daily if you need to.

Prayer

Heavenly Father, I repent of every sin that I have committed before you. I release every lie of the enemy that has tried to keep me away from you. You said if I draw near to you, you will draw near to me. As I attempt to get close to you, let me know you are here and show me the areas where I have a veil on before you. Help me to be transparent and vulnerable with you. When I drift away from you, convict me to return to you. Give me a godly sorrow that leads to repentance. Speak Lord, for I am listening. I make room for you.

In Jesus name, Amen.

Acceptable Priesthood

Day 4: Leviticus 9

[1]But Nadav and Avihu... offered unauthorized fire before *Adonai*, something he had not ordered them to do. [2] ...so that they died in the presence of *Adonai*.

Leviticus 10:1-2 CJB

One phrase that I have grown to despise is "come as you are". This phrase is used by evangelical (soul winning, not denominational) christians to persuade potential converts to come to God despite their current physical state. While I understand what it is trying to express, I fail to find such language in the Bible. I do not believe someone has to change their exterior before they come into a relationship with God; however, I do not believe they can "come as they are". Jesus said, "If any man come to Me, he must pick up his cross, deny himself, and follow Me" (Luke 9:23). This was how Jesus evangelized. While He told potential followers, "I will make you" into something physically eventually, He made sure to prepare them mentally (Matthew 4:19). They did not have to change physically, but they had to alter their mentality. This is what the word repent means: to have a change of heart! In this case, you cannot come as you are. You have to come with a **changed** mindset that will alter your outside eventually, not before, or immediately after, meeting Christ. As you read the gospels, you will find that Jesus did not sugarcoat His expectations to build an army of soldiers who were not mentally prepared. He clearly listed His standards so they can understand what they were about to experience. They were introduced to the life of the priesthood: a life of sacrificing yourself and your flesh.

Priesthood Has Standards

Remember, the introduction of this book pointed out three categories of people: the churchgoer, the kingdom citizen, and the Priest. Each category points out a different level of intimacy with God. The Priest is differentiated by the strict requirements associated with its function. If you read Leviticus 21-22, you will find that Priests had to follow a lot of rules. They could not do whatever they wanted, but there was a strict protocol they had to observe. This includes the way they conducted their lives and the physical sacrifices they offered unto God. Because we are the under the dispensation of Grace (post the death of Jesus Christ), we do not have to follow the same practice; however, we have to observe the same principle. God does not accept whatever we give Him. God only accepts what meets His standards.

If you read Leviticus 9 and the first 2 verses of Leviticus 10, you will find a juxtaposition. These are two contrasting situations placed directly next to each other for the purpose of making a point. Because the Bible is a God- breathed work of art, it requires our critical, rhetorical analysis to fully comprehend everything it is saying to us. In His wisdom, the Lord shows us two sacrifices in two adjacent chapters that are polar opposites. In Leviticus 9, you find God giving clear instructions to Moses that Aaron executed to the fullest extent. The sacrifice ended with the manifested presence, or Glory, of God. In Leviticus

10, you find a sacrifice that is described as "unauthorized".

Did God Authorize That?

There is so much we can learn from the sacrifice of Aaron's sons. The number one thing is, **they did something that God did not ask them for.** As a Priest you cannot operate from your opinion. You have to function from the leading of the Spirit of God. It is very dangerous to engage in a spiritual activity without the license of God. This is what Jesus meant when He said, "anybody who enters not by the door [Himself] to the sheep is a thief and a robber" (John 10:1). You cannot do as you feel, but you must do as He said. Just because it is godly, it does not mean it is God ordained at that time. For example, Paul was forbidden to preach in an area (Acts 16:6). It is not about doing godly stuff, but doing what God ordained. This is why the priesthood is so important. Soaking in His presence is the key to attaining prophetic instruction of what to do, when to do it, and how to do it.

The sacrifice of Aaron's sons reveal their heart before God and their attitude towards the things of God. The juxtaposition reveals that they tried to replicate what was experienced in the previous chapter. They wanted similar results but they did not follow suit with the same steps. They microwaved the process. In Leviticus 9, God sent His own fire and burned up their sacrifices. In Leviticus 10, they set their own fire without any sacrifice. You cannot experience the glory of the priesthood without the sacrifice of the priesthood. The fire was unauthorized because it attempted to be of Him without coming from Him. Back then, they offered physical sacrifices. Today, the sacrifice is our own life (Romans 12:1). I wonder how many people are unauthorized sacrifices before God because they attempt to be of Him without really coming from Him (or from a consistent surrender in His presence).

You are from God if you obey God (John 8:31). You only move when He wants you to move. When He sets a standard of what He desires in your personal life, you do not look for loopholes or shortcuts. Instead, you fully take on the challenge of doing exactly what He said. If God set a standard for you, it is because

He knows it is attainable, bearable, and beneficial (1 John 5:3). Do not neglect His instruction for personal convenience. An example of this is seen in Scripture. God demanded that the sacrifices of the priesthood must be offered in the Temple, or the place He chose for His name (Deuteronomy 12:11,14). In the book of Hosea, God shared that He was grieved because, "They sacrifice on the mountain peaks and offer incense on the hills under oaks, poplars and pistachio trees; **because they give good shade**" (Hosea 4:13 CJB). Instead of going where God said, they went where it was comfortable. Comfortability is the complete opposite of sacrifice. It is these type of sacrifices that God does not accept. Again, because we are under grace, we do not have to physically go to a Temple because we are the Temple of God (1 Corinthians 6:19). While we do not have to follow the practice, we still must learn from the principle. I cannot give God any type of sacrifice that I feel. I must meet the standard that He has.

We will talk about this more, but it must be understood that as you build an altar, God is not accepting any and everything from it. He only accepts what He has authorized or asked for.

Incorporating This Into Your Prayer Life

As you build an altar before the Lord, ask Him how He wants it to be built. Do not pray for a long time because someone else does. Ask Him how long He wants you to pray for. Do not pray for less than that because it is convenient for you. Ask Him for clear instruction on what to read in the Scripture. Exercise Proverbs 3:5-6. Ask God what to eat, what to wear, where to go, and what to say when you get there.

Reflection Questions

1. What standards does God have for my personal life in this season?

2. Was there a time when God gave me a standard and I did not keep it? What can I do differently to avoid this phenomenon from repeating itself?

Prayer

Heavenly Father, I repent of not keeping your standards. I no longer want to chose convenience over obedience. Help me Holy Spirit to desire and carry out the standards You have put on My life. Convict me and constantly remind me of what is required for me to walk out my individual priesthood before You. Empower me to push beyond my feelings. I thank you for your grace and mercy that gives me a fresh chance daily to try again.

In Jesus name, Amen.

Pure Priesthood

Day 5: MALACHI 1

He will sit, testing and purifying the silver; He will purify the sons of Levi, refining them like gold and silver, so that they can bring offerings to *Adonai* uprightly.

Malachi 3:3 CJB

Yesterday, we spoke about an acceptable priesthood. We identified that God has standards for sacrifices. He does not want any and everything, but He wants what He authorized. He has requirements for what we offer as a Priest and if we do not follow those requirements, He will not accept what we are giving Him. A major standard of the priesthood back then that *still* applies to us today is **PURITY.** God wants every sacrifice to be pure: clean from any toxins.

When they offered animal sacrifices in the Old Testament, whatever they presented to God had to be *pristine*. It had to be in mint condition. They could not offer an animal that had a bruise, blemish, or broken body part (Leviticus 22:22). If an animal was deformed in any way, it was now considered defiled because it was not in **its original condition**. A Priest lives a life of worship, because worship is ultimately sacrifice. When people offered animal sacrifices in the Old Testament, that was their way of worshipping. The words "worship" and "sacrifice" are synonymous. If God has a standard for worship, He has that same standard for our sacrifice. God said that those who worship Him, must do so in spirit and in truth (John 4:24). I want us to dig deeper into this terminology.

"Spirit" and "truth" are not just ways one can worship, but they are two **original** aspects of the creation of man. Human beings are triune: spirit, soul, and body (1 Thessalonians 5:23). When God created man in Genesis 1:26, He did not create their body or soul (that happened in Genesis 2:7). The original form of man is spirit. Adam and Eve lived in what I like to call the "Formed Righteous Era" (You can learn more about this in Chapter 3 of my book: *Unlocking The Joshua Anointing*). This means that they were the only people who started off their lives sinless. They entered the earth in a state of absolute truth. They were free from the lies of Satan and sin. **Purity is not only cleanliness but it is also originality.** When God asks us to worship in Spirit and in Truth, the original way He formulated mankind, this is Him asking for pure, original, more so the **standard** type of worship. I want us to think of Adam and Eve because they had a **level of purity** we will not attain until we go to

Heaven. Before the serpent, they were for God and God alone.

What Are Your Motives?

The Serpent convinced Eve to eat the fruit by enticing her motives: the reasons why someone commits an action. Eve ate it because "she wanted to be like gods" (Genesis 3:5-6). The enemy tries to put his desires on us. The same way he wanted to be like God, he made Eve have a similar desire (Isaiah 14:14). She was supposed to eat the fruit in the garden for nourishment, but instead she was eating it to usurp God. The enemy will make you do a "harmless" thing with the wrong intentions. The wrong intentions can make a harmless thing horrible for you.

God does not want your worship if you do it with the wrong heart. The Kingdom is not only about what you do, but why you do it. Remember, yesterday we discussed Aaron's sons. They offered a sacrifice but God did not accept it. **It was because their motives were not pure.** They did it out of comparison instead of worship. Every action we commit has a spirit influencing it (Jeremiah 10:23). God is more concerned about the motive behind our actions instead of the action itself (1 Samuel 16:7;Proverbs 16:2). Jesus shared that some people only pray and fast to get attention (Matthew 6:5). Before we move further, I have to ask you, **"why do you want to be a Priest?"**. Are your motives in the right place?

IT IS NOT ABOUT YOU

The priesthood is a life of sacrifice. On Day 1, we emphasized that this process is about killing your flesh. I am here to warn you. **Do not engage in building an altar to build your own name.** Every altar has a name! You are not building your own altar. You are building His altar! In Malachi 1, God kept saying "my altar" to denote that it belongs to Him and not to the people who sacrifice on it (Malachi 1:7). The altar is not for the advancement of man but the exaltation of God. However, if God is exalted, it also advances man due to them getting closer to God (John 12:32). The motive should be to exalt God and get closer to Him. God also shared how tired He was of polluted sacrifices. Any time we give something to God for our personal gain, it is now a polluted sacrifice. While we want to operate as a Priest, prophet, and a king, our dominion is not for self magnification, it is for His magnification. If you are making the priesthood about you, God does not want anything from you.

God Wants A Pure You

The biggest sacrifice that you will have to lay on the altar is your heart (Joel 2:13). You will have to do this on a consistent basis. When David sinned against the Lord by sleeping with Bathsheba, he did not ask God to purify his lustful actions. He prayed, "Create in me a **Clean Heart**" (Psalm 51:10). For this reason, Malachi 3:3 does not say God vowed to refine the sacrifices of the sons of Levi. While their sacrifices were polluted, His focus was not on cleaning **what they offered**. Instead, God was focused on cleaning **those who offered**. God vowed to refine the sons of Levi themselves. Further evidence of this is seen when God shares that He desires "mercy and not sacrifice" (Hosea 6:6;Matthew 9:13). Mercy means "kindness": a characteristic of a clean heart. God was emphasizing that He would rather people offer a clean heart instead of routine, religious sacrifices from a corrupt heart. He vowed to clean the hearts of the sons of Levi because **a clean heart will redeem a dirty life**. David is the best example of this. Although David committed plenty of sins, God still kept His covenant with him and protected his generations because of his heart (Isaiah 37:35).

Incorporating This Into Your Prayer Life

As you build an altar before the Lord, make sure it is for the right reasons. Ask yourself, "do I have any ulterior motives?". Be transparent! Are you seeking God so you can grow in a gift? Are you trying to prove a point in ministry? Pray against this so it does not limit you. Ask God to reveal to you anything that you do not know about.

Reflection Questions

1. What are some wrong motives that I have?

2. What strategies can I implement to clean my heart?

Prayer

Heavenly Father, I want to have a pure heart before you. Create in me a clean heart and renew a right spirit within me. As I build this altar, I want to sacrifice myself and I want to only exalt your name. I bind any demonic spirit that tries to persuade me to seek you for the wrong reason. Holy Spirit help me. With you, all things are possible.

In Jesus Name, Amen.

Purifying Your Priesthood

Day 6: JOHN 15

³ Now ye are clean through the word which I have spoken unto you.

John 15:3 KJV

The title of today's devotional is not a typo. While yesterday's title (Pure Priesthood) may be similar to today's (Purifying Your Priesthood), they are not the same. "Pure" is an adjective and "Purifying" is a verb. After learning that our priesthood must be pure, today, we will learn **how** to obtain that purity before the Lord.

Consider David, who we discussed yesterday. Many people think sleeping with Bathsheba and murdering Uriah was David's only sins. However, David committed a list of grievances against God. David was a liar (1 Samuel 21:2). He also violated the Old Testament law of the priesthood by eating the shewbread off of the altar in the Temple (1 Samuel 21:6). He joined the army of his enemy and almost killed off his own people so he can be "protected" by the enemy (1 Samuel 27-28). He also murdered a bunch of armies that God did not tell him to kill (1 Samuel 27). God tells David that he cannot build a house before God because he has way too much blood on his hands (1 Chronicles 28:3). Read all of 1 Samuel if you do not believe me! David was a sinful man! Yet, he was the only man recorded as one after God's own heart. God spared an entire city because of His covenant with His servant David (2 Kings 19:34). How is this possible?

What Is The Heart?

In order to understand the phrase "David was a man after God's own heart", one must comprehend the biblical meaning of the word "heart". It is way more than an organ in the body. It is defined as the seat of the soul and ultimately, the proper way to describe a man (Proverbs 27:19) It is where the mind (thoughts), will (desires), and emotions (feelings) are found. David was a man who pursued what God thought, wanted, and felt. The heart is the origin of everything we experience (Proverbs 4:23); consequently, it is even the source of what we say (Matthew 12:34). The speech of a person is a tool to measure their heart. That means if David constantly pursued God's heart, David sought out what God was saying.

One famous phrase that repeats itself in the book of 1 and 2 Samuel is, "And David enquired of the Lord" (1 Samuel 23:2,4; 1 Samuel 30:8; 2 Samuel 2:1; 2 Samuel 5:19,23; 2 Samuel 21:1). I personally found 7 times where David asked God, "what should I do?". This means David made room for the word of the Lord. That word is what makes your heart pure!

The Bible is a critical component for the believer. There is nothing more important in the Christian faith. The Bible, also known as the word of God, is God Himself (John 1:1). If you do not read your Bible, and seek out the proceeding (prophetic) Word of God that points back to the Bible, you are disconnected from God. You are disconnected from the heart of God.

David was always in pursuit of the Word of God. Psalm 119 (the longest chapter of the Bible with 176 verses), written by David, is an outpouring of David's deep desire for the Word of God. A famous verse from that passage is "How can a young man keep his way pure? By guarding it according to your word" (Psalm 119:9 CJB). In other words, the only way to keep your heart and priesthood pure is by guarding it with the Word of God. This includes seeking the Word of God, studying it to develop understanding, and obeying it to the best of your ability. Today is for the person who has been slacking on their Bible Study. You cannot be a Priest without the Word of God. God chastised the Priests in Hosea by sharing, "My people are destroyed for lack of knowledge: because thou hast rejected knowledge, I will also reject thee, that **thou shalt be no Priest to me**" (Hosea 4:6 KJV). They were rejected as Priests because they rejected the Word. Unless you take heed to the

Word of God, you can never execute the priesthood correctly.

Your heart is cleaned by the word. In John 15, Jesus explains to His disciples that, as they produce for Him, He is constantly pruning them. This lets me know a few things:

1. I do not have to be entirely clean to start the process. If Jesus prunes us after we bear fruit, that means we are not completely clean to begin with. This is why Day 3 emphasized approaching the Throne of Grace boldly! We cannot put up a veil of guilt back up when Jesus split it permanently!

2. Pruning is a continual process. One altar call does not make us clean. One fast does not make

us clean. Reading the word one time or praying one time does not make us clean. Will I make more mistakes along the way? Absolutely! Does that mean I stop my pursuit? Absolutely not! People think a righteous man is a person who never falls; however, the Bible records a righteous man as one who falls seven times but GETS BACK UP (Proverbs 24:16). Righteousness is not the absence of falling. It is the by-product of a constant pursuit despite failures along the way. David kept getting back up! If you stopped pursuing, I challenge you to get back up.

Make Room For The Word

From today, you can see that the Word is a prominent pillar of our priesthood. It is actually the foundation of everything we do in the Kingdom of God (Matthew 7:24-27). If you try to grow in God without the Word of God, you are building a house with a weak foundation. You are building something that will not last. Do not be that person! As you indulge in the Word of God, you are cleaning your heart. Jesus said our hearts are cleaned by the Word (John 15:3). Do not give me an excuse! Get into the Word so the Word can clean you! There are several ways you can get the Word into you:

- Make a daily schedule such as a plan on the Bible app

- Join a Bible study group with your friends or church

- Listen to Gospel Music

- Watch Sermons instead of Secular TV all of the time

Incorporating This Into Your Prayer Life

As you build an altar before the Lord, begin to pray scriptures. As you pray about certain topics, declare scriptures that relate to those topics. Research them if you have to, and then pray them out after you collected all of them. This is known as a prayer strategy. I learned this from the three gatekeepers I mentioned at the end of this book's dedication! It is also a great way to recite and memorize the Word of God! This helps you hide the word in your heart.

Reflection Questions

1. How often do I read the Bible? Is there a way I can incorporate more scripture?

2. What can I do to hold myself accountable in terms of reading my Word (ex. Bible Study Partner, Study Group, Bible App Streaks)?

Prayer

Heavenly Father, I thank you for your mercy. I want to read more of your Word. That is the only way that I experience more of you and develop a pure heart before you. Holy Spirit, make me hungry for the word of the Lord. Convict me to desire you more than anything else and empower me to push through the times when I may be tired or become bored. I depend on you. Grant me your wisdom.

In Jesus name, Amen.

Bible Study Advice

I have two tips for people who want to go deeper Bible study but do not know where to start.

1. **Read chronologically.** Start at Matthew and read the entire New Testament in order. Then start at Genesis and read the entire Old Testament in order. This allows you to get context and understand what is going on when you come across a particular verse.

2. **Read categorically.** Especially as you write prayer strategies, look up all the scriptures pertaining to a certain word or a topic. This allows you to get a complete sense

of what the Bible has to say about a certain thing. I use the Bible app for this. Go to the search bar and look up a word like "love". Every verse about that topic will show up. For paper Bibles, use the index or concordance at the back of it, if it has one. Study Bibles are best for this.

Prioritized Priesthood

Day 7: GENESIS 4

and Hevel [Abel] too brought from the first-born of his sheep, including their fat. *Adonai* accepted Hevel [Abel] and his offering but did not accept Kayin [Cain] and his offering.

Genesis 4:4-5 CJB

You are officially on the last day of establishing your priesthood! We have discussed principles such as alteration, repentance, pressing in His presence, and purification. The last foundational principle that we will discuss is the concept of "first", or priority. If the Kingdom of God runs on anything, it runs on the idea of precedence (Matthew 6:33). If you plan on pursuing the priesthood, it must be priority for you!

Genesis 4 describes two brothers who both came before God with a sacrifice. God accepted Abel's sacrifice but He denied Cain's. While many people have different reasons as to why Cain was rejected, I believe the answer is right before our eyes. The Bible records that Cain brought any fruit, but Abel brought the firstborn of his sheep. Abel's sacrifice shows us a standard that God has in the Kingdom of God.

The Standard Of The Tithe

No, this is not a financial handbook. I do not have a Cash App that I want you to send a seed to. However, giving is another aspect of the priesthood that teaches us the importance of priority. In Malachi 4, God sharply rebuked the children of Israel because they withheld the tithe. The tithe is known as giving God the **first 10%** of your increase (For them it was their crops/cattle. For us today it is our paychecks). Let me make this clear for you. If you make $100 and you buy a meal for $10, then you go and give God $10, that is not a tithe. This is controversial for many. If the tithe is 10%, and $10 is 10% of 100, why is the $10 not a tithe? A tithe is not just any 10%, but it is the **first 10%.** Some people think it is only about the amount, but it is also about the **order**. The order of your sacrifice reveals the priority of your heart.

For many, they pay all their bills and give God what is left over. They basically tell God, my bills are my priority. If I do not have enough to pay my bills, I am unable to pay my tithe. This is how Cain presented his sacrifice. He did not give God the first, but he gave God whatever was left over. I can imagine Cain taking the first for himself for dinner, and then giving to God after he was already satisfied. So many approach their priesthood this way.

People do whatever they need to do, and give God the back end. With 24 hours in a day, we do everything else and save the last "hour" before bed for God. Then, we cannot even give him the full hour because we are tired from everything else. As a result, we fall asleep while praying or reading our Bible. How do you love God more than everything else, but He is the last person to get some of your energy? Have you ever had a "talking stage" crush before? Did you leave them for the last of your day? Absolutely not! Often times, they are the first person you talk to when you wake up! Social Media tends to be the first thing we go to in the morning. We only pray when we need something. If life is good, God tends to be last. This is not the way it should be.

Put God First

This is not a toxic approach to your relationship with God. I did not tell you to give God your ALL. God does not ask for the entire paycheck or increase (at least not for everybody), but only the first 10%. As a full time college student (who has worked two jobs while running a youth ministry and writing books), I understand that there is things we have to do. I am not telling you to forget everything else and focus on God alone. I believe God has anointed us to prosper educationally, financially, and in the area of family especially. On the contrary, I do not believe God wants to be forgotten in the midst of all the blessings He has given us. God wants to be remembered. Our blessings should not be an excuse to neglect God, but it should be an encouragement to seek God.

As Jesus was doing ministry, He asked some people to follow Him, but they wanted to do other things first (Luke 9:57-62). Before they followed Jesus, they said "let me first" pursue other things. You can miss Jesus by saving Him for last. In Matthew 22, Jesus invited people to feast with Him but their priority was their own things. The Bible records each man going to "his farm or his merchandise" (Matthew 22:4-5). One the first day, I told you that the pursuit of the priesthood is ultimately the sacrifice of you. On the seventh day, I remind you: there has to be a sacrifice of you! Am I saying that you will not get anything? Absolutely not! You will receive something, but you can longer be your everything. You can no longer be your priority. God has to be first. The Bible tells us to seek God first and everything else that we need will be supplied (Matthew 6:33). You do not need to pursue self to experience the best version of yourself. If you seek your life you will lose it, but if you lay it down you will gain it (Matthew 16:25). Putting God first is not an omission of benefitting self, it is only removing self from the place of priority. A failure to put God first led to mayhem in Cain's life. Because he did not prioritize the priest-hood, he opened the door for all kinds of spirits to come in and hurt him: rejection, anger, murder, and pride. Your priesthood is ultimately protection for you. This will be continued in part two of the develop-mental devotional series.

Incorporating This Into Your Prayer Life

As you build an altar before the Lord, seek God first. David said he sought God early in the morning (Psalm 63:1). Jesus said that God woke Him up morning by morning (Isaiah 50:4). By now, if you put everything in this devotional to practice, you should have built a stronger prayer life. Put that prayer life above all else. Do not go a day without seeking God first. If you forget, do not go to bed without doing it at all. Remember, quality over quantity. Something is better than nothing. However, do not slack on your priesthood! Put it first and build on it.

Reflection Questions

1. Do I truly put God first? How can I continue putting Him first or rectify the times when I have not?

2. How has my prayer life built because of this book? What will I do differently now? Send this answer to kirklandayeisha@gmail.com if possible.

Prayer

Heavenly Father, I thank you for helping me to build my prayer life. I want to stay in your presence. I want to go deeper. I want to see more. Let the end of this book not be a break in my priesthood, but the start of my personal priesthood. Give me more revelation about what it means to be a Priest. I thank you for using this book to draw me close.

In Jesus Name, Amen.